The Snail Cookbook
Recipes from both sides of the Pyrenees

Walter Gunn

*For Zenaida Quinones de Leon Vidal-Quadras
who introduced me to the delicious caracoles of Restaurante 8S in Ainsa*

The Snail Cookbook
Photography - Walter Gunn
Copyright © 2012 by Walter Gunn

The Snail Cookbook

The Snail Cookbook - Walter Gunn

Contents:

Introduction	4 - 7
Buying or collecting; confining	8 - 9
Cleaning, pre-cooking and a cosmetic footnote	10 - 15
Recipes from the Spanish and Catalan side of the Pyrenees	16 - 31
Recipes from the French side of the Pyrenees	32 - 47
Sauces and accompaniments	48 - 64

Coclea   Chiociola   Caracol

Introduction:

Snails, not known for their turn of speed, are one of the few wild animals I can outpace. Though that's not the reason I cook them. It's much simpler than that; they make very, very good eating and if you're a gardener and a cook, it's an eminently logical, and environmentally sound, way of wreaking revenge on the little buggers. Considerable social advantage can be taken with the championing of snail control by consumption rather than by chemicals; there's moral high-ground up for grabs here.

You may not be aware that the common garden snail *(Helix aspersa)* found in Great Britain is perfectly edible and excellent. Indeed, there are areas of France and certainly in the Spanish Pyrenees that consider them preferable in flavour and tenderness to the much larger escargot *(Helix pomatia)* - these are the ones usually dished up in French restaurants. The book features recipes for both the common garden snail *(Helix aspersa)* and the Roman snail *(Helix pomatia)*.

The Spanish and French have markedly different approaches to snail cookery. As a reasonable generalisation, the French tend towards stuffings and light sauces; the Spanish lean in the direction of rich robust stews and roasts. On both sides though, many recipes merely contain minor iterations of others very similar. The Snail Cookbook whittles these down to the essential few. The recipes and information on preparation will give the reader all the necessary know-how - and if they cook every recipe, they will gain sufficient experience to experiment for themselves.

A little etymology. To my ears, the Spanish name caracol has a much more appetising sound to it than snail or escargot. In Spanish, caracol can also mean spiral or curl. While the sweet sounding caracolillo, means kiss-curl – isn't that nice? And, while on the subject, horses, when they are prancing about, are said to be making caracoles. The word has even entered the English language; in Dressage, a half turn to the left or right made by the horse and rider is also known as a Caracole.

The Snail Cookbook - Walter Gunn

Cargol   Escargòlh   Escargot

At first glance the word caracol seems to bear little relationship to escargot. Dig a little deeper and you can trace the etymology from caracol in the Spanish Iberian Peninsular through to the Catalan; cargol. Travelling then round the eastern end of the Pyrenees to Occitan speaking France you have escargòlh and this leads to, as it is known throughout greater France; escargot. Be that as it may, I'd lay good money that the root of the word caracol came to Spain with the Roman Legions. The Italian word for snails is chiocciola and that is only a small evolution from the Latin coclea.

So, the sequence goes like this:
    Coclea; Chiociola; Caracol; Cargol; Escargòlh; Escargot.
    Latin; Italian; Spanish; Catalan; Occitan; French.

Reading old recipe books written in Gascon, you will also come across other occitan teasers; Escaraouiches and Escaravixas - try saying those with a mouthful.

As well as coclea, Latin uses the word limax for snail. The French reserve a corruption of this for the garden slug; limace. These are not eaten.

The Oxford English Dictionary submits that *snail* comes from *Old English*; snægl and snegl. *Old Saxon*; snegil. *Middle Low German*; sneil. *Old High German*; snegil, or, *Old Norse*; snigill. These are not pretty words and probably account for the English not having a history of snail eating. A plate of snigills *indeed*.

Popular opinion, so often misleading, would have it that France is the premier snail eating country of the world. As an observation from someone who has lived on both sides of the Pyrenees - several years on each - it is clear that the Spanish eat many more snails per head than the French. And, for the

snægl   snegl   snegil   sneil   snigill   snail

Coclea   Chiociola   Caracol

introduction continued...

record, more myth dispelling observations are these; since living in France I have heard 'Ooh La la' uttered in public on just one occasion and 'Zut Alors' never.

The French have a wealth of excellent recipes for *'les escargots'*, and ,as with most subjects, have strong opinions about the advantages of one sort over another and the best ways of preparing them. Strong opinions, or passion if you like, have been known to lead to excess and occasionally insanity and one wonders about the mental stability of the creators of these little gems: *Escargot Ravioli*, *Tomates Cerises Farcies aux Escargots* - that's *Cherry Tomatoes Stuffed with Snails*, *Vol-au-vents aux Escargots* and, the dubiously sounding; *Escargots en Surprise*. These recipes will not be included in this book, though I might write another entitled *'Les Escargots for the Desperate Chef'*. The French stop just short of praying to snails. Over the Pyrenean watershed things are little more intense.

In Spain, there are fiestas celebrating just about anyone and anything, including of course, those for snails – the Caracoladas. To be a little more accurate, they are not so much dedicated to them, as to eating them.

In Sobrarbe, where I lived for a few years, there's a particular evening in May when they hold their Caracolada, and if then, you were to go to the medieval square of Ainsa you'd find cauldrons of caracoles steaming away and alongside them, great pots of what appear to be creamed potato – in fact it's a special mayonnaise called *Ajoaciete*. It is made with creamed potato; egg yolks; garlic and olive oil. The fiesta makes a wonderful evening: soft warm air - though sometimes at Ainsa's altitude it can be nippy - music, traditional dancing, food and wine and, for all this there's no official charge – just a few honesty boxes to accept what can be afforded.

As quaint and homely as it is, Ainsa's Caracolada is small stuff compared with that of the Catalan town of Lerida. On one gut-busting week-end they get through something in the order of *3 tonnes of snails*.

The Snail Cookbook - Walter Gunn

Cargol Escargòlh Escargot

A huge vat of 'Caracoles Aragonese' at Ainsa's Caracolada

snægl   snegl   snegil   sneil   snigill   snail

Coclea   Chiociola   Caracol

Buying or collecting, confining

In markets and those shops that sell them, live snails are usually sold by weight - a handy reckoner is that 1/2 kg is more-or-less equal to about 80. Should you prefer the thrill of the hunt, they are best collected after dark on damp evenings in spring, summer and early autumn. They are said to develop best within a temperature range of 18 to 20°C

and an accompanying humidity of between 70 and 80%. This probably accounts for them rarely being collected during the winter hibernation when their condition is generally not at its best.

To accommodate their increasing size during development, snails add a new section to the shell's mouth. So you may come across some where this part is still soft; if you do, discard them, because there is a tendency for the shells to break up during cooking.

The Snail Cookbook - Walter Gunn

Cargol   Escargòlh   Escargot

Confinement:

The period of confinement exists simply to rid the snails of any toxins they may have gained from eating poisonous plants. I've met those who buck this advice and think it unnecessary: by far the greater consensus advises their isolation from between 5 to 10 days: in France, some advocate as much as a month.

The best way to corral them is to put the harvested snails into a bucket or similar container - *see page over for my set-up*. Whatever type of container you use, there will need to be a few small ventilation holes in it, and, you will also need to cover it to curb escapees - it's worth putting a weight on top of the lid. Snails, as a group, are surprisingly strong - I've seen them shift, with apparent ease, a piece of thick plywood before making a dash for the hills. To keep them healthy and clean, swill them and their containers, every couple of days with cold fresh water.

As always, there's quite a split of opinion: do you, or don't you, feed them during confinement?   Some say; not at all, some feed them lettuce or cabbage leaves and herbs such as thyme - they love fennel by the way. Many give bran, flour or oatmeal. It is a fact that the well-fed ones are plumper. So, bearing this in mind, I settled for what seems to me to be the best of both worlds; I feed them for 4 days on whatever I can get my hands on in the way of cabbage and lettuce leaves, and I starve them until they are no longer producing pooh - this depoohing phase takes around 7 days - it's practical and very effective. Treated this way, they remain in top condition while at the end of the starving period they've rid themselves of all bodily waste and potential toxins.

snægl   snegl   snegil   sneil   snigill   snail

Coclea   Chiociola   Caracol

Cleaning:

If there is a stage that's going to put you off eating snails, this could be it. Now is when you are going to rid them of most of their slime. And, while we're on this slightly less savoury aspect of the process, it is interesting to note that you will be washing away something that in previous times was used, by the unscrupulous I should add, to thicken milk, which was then passed off as cream. There's a marvellous passage in Tobias Smollet's; *Humphrey Clinker*, where Matt Bramble, in one of his letters, writes of the worst milk being thickened and being sold as cream after having, amongst other things, been *'lowered with hot water, frothed with bruised snails, carried through the streets in open pails'*. I won't quote the rest of the passage, it's just possible that you'd never touch milk or cream again.

I've come across a variety of cleaning methods in the Pyrenees all aimed at achieving a mucous free kitchen. What follows, are my own adaptations of both Catalan and Aragonese methods. In my opinion, concerning the recipes in this book, they give the best results and, achieve them with the least effort. Assuming a harvest of between 40 and 50 snails, here's what to do for all the recipes except 'Roast Snails' and 'Snails a la Restaurant 88' - their cleaning method is to be found on their respective pages.

1. After giving the snails a good swilling off under the cold tap, put them into a washing-up bowl or bucket. Add to them a large handful of salt and about 3 tablespoons of white wine vinegar.

2. Taking care not to damage the shells, vigorously rub them between your hands – this has a similar effect on the snails to the bruising mentioned in the Humphrey Clinker quote above; it makes them froth and give up their slime - I would like to come up with a more pleasant terms than slime or mucous; but that's what it is though. It's a messy business and attempts at word sanitisation have been resisted.

Cargol   Escargòlh   Escargot

My set-up for confining snails: 2 upturned plastic bins, stones to weigh them down all stood on fine wire mesh - white wine vinegar and salt standing-by ready for cleaning

3.   It won't take long before they are giving up loads of mucous - a minute or so. When the giving up is slackening, rinse the snails under the cold tap and repeat the salt and vinegaring process at least 2 more times or until there is only a small amount of mucous being emitted - the rest will disappear during initial cooking.

4.   Finally rinse them again with cold water. They are now ready for their initial cooking.

A cosmetic footnote: There is an upside to snail mucous, and it's this: it is unbelievably good for treating cracked and chapped hands - I know of no better. A couple of sessions of bare-handed de-sliming, performed miracles on my winter crevassed fingers - from '*Elephant Man*' to fully restored in two weeks.

snægl   snegl   snegil   sneil   snigill   snail

Coclea   Chiociola   Caracol

Pre-cooking:

With the exception of the recipes for *Roast Snails, Snails a la Restaurant 88* and pre-cooked canned snails, a 2-stage process of pre-cooking is carried out. Firstly, over a low heat, they are placed in cold water which is slowly raised to the boil. The reason for starting with cold water is a very practical one. If you were to throw the snails into boiling water they would immediately retract into the furthest recesses of their shells, making it very difficult to remove them later. By putting them in cold water first, their heads remain outside the shell and, when cooked, they can be easily twanged out with a toothpick or cocktail stick. Following the initial pre-cook stage, they are once more cooked in whatever stock advised by the recipe being followed. Using live snails, the pre-cooking methods assume a harvest of between 40 to 50.

Method 1. The classic courte-bouillon: In French cuisine, courte-bouillon is indispensable. It is used for poaching fish, chicken, veal, shellfish and, of course, snails. It is the base stock for sauce blanche and many potages. If you double or triple the quantities advised below, you can freeze what is not required for the snails, or store it for a short time in a corked bottle in the refrigerator. If you choose to do this, you will have the opportunity for trying your hand at poaching fish or chicken at some other time.

Courte-bouillon ingredients - makes 1 Lt:

50g	Carrot - cut into small cubes.
50g	Onion - finely chopped.
2 to 3	Celery or Kintsai leaves.
600ml	Water.
200ml	White wine vinegar.
200ml	Dry white wine.
1/2	Bay leaf.
1 sprig	Parsley - broad leaved.
1 sprig	Fresh thyme - or a small pinch of dried
1/2 teaspoon	Sea salt - if using fine table salt, use less.
10	Black peppercorns.

Cargol　　Escargòlh　　Escargot

Making the court-bouillon:
1. In a lidded pan, put the herbs, salt, peppercorns and carrots into the cold water, and over a medium/low heat, bring to a gentle simmer. Lower the heat and continue very gently simmering for 5 or 6 mins.
2. Add the onions and simmer for another 5 mins.
3. Add the wine and vinegar, and simmer, still covered, for a further 20 minutes.
4. Strain and discard the vegetables. The court-bouillon is now ready for use.

Pre-cooking in the court-bouillon:
1. Put the snails in a saucepan with 1 Lt cold water.
2. Put a lid on the saucepan, and over a medium to low heat, bring slowly to the boil.
3. When the water boils, take off the heat and wash the snails under cold water.
4. Return them to the saucepan with 1 Lt of the court-bouillon.
5. Bring to the boil, lower the heat and simmer for 1 hour.
6. Take out the snails; they are now ready for use.

snægl　　snegl　　snegil　　sneil　　snigill　　snail

Coclea   Chiociola   Caracol

Method 2.

For pre-cooking:
Garden snails in Aragonese sauce.
Garden snails with rabbit.
Garden snails with chorizo, apple and cider.
Garden snails with thyme and parsley.

Method 2: pre-cooking ingredients:

2	Cloves of garlic - with peel left on and cut ¾ of the way across.
1 teaspoon	Dried thyme.
½ teaspoon	Dried oregano.
1 teaspoon	Sea salt - if using fine table salt, use less.
1	Bay leaf.
1	Small chilli pepper - Guindilla.

Method 2: pre-cooking:

1. Put the snails in a saucepan with 1 Lt cold water.
2. Put a lid on the saucepan, and over a medium to low heat, bring slowly to the boil.
3. When the water boils, take off the heat and wash the snails under cold water.
4. Return them to the saucepan with a fresh litre of cold water to which you have added all the ingredients.
5. Bring to the boil, lower the heat and simmer for 1 hour.
6. Take out the snails, and - for some of the recipes - reserve the liquid for later use.
7. They are now ready for whichever of the recipes you have chosen to cook.

The Snail Cookbook - Walter Gunn

Cargol   Escargòlh   Escargot

Method 3.   For pre-cooking:
Garden snails with chocolate.

Method 3: pre-cooking ingredients:
4 sprigs   Mint - around 10cms each.
1 teaspoon Sea salt - if using fine table salt, use less.

Method 3: pre-cooking:
1. Put the snails in a saucepan with 1 Lt cold water.
2. Put a lid on the saucepan, and over a medium to low heat, bring slowly to the boil.
3. When the water boils, take off the heat and wash the snails with cold water.
4. Return them to the saucepan with a fresh litre of cold water, the mint and the salt.
5. Bring to the boil, lower the heat and simmer for 1 hour.
6. Take out the snails. They are now ready for cooking 'Garden snails with chocolate'.

snægl   snegl   snegil   sneil   snigill   snail

The Snail Cookbook

The Snail Cookbook - Walter Gunn

Recipes from the Spanish side of the Pyrenees:

Garden snails with:

Hot chilli pepper & coñac - a la restaurant 88 in Ainsa	18 - 19
Aragonese sauce	20 - 21
Rabbit, green peppers and white wine	22 - 23
2 methods of roasting	24 - 25
Chorizo, apple and cider	26 - 27
Thyme and parsley	28 - 29
Chocolate, hazel nuts and chilli	30 - 31

The Spanish side - Caracoles a la restaurant 88 Ainsa

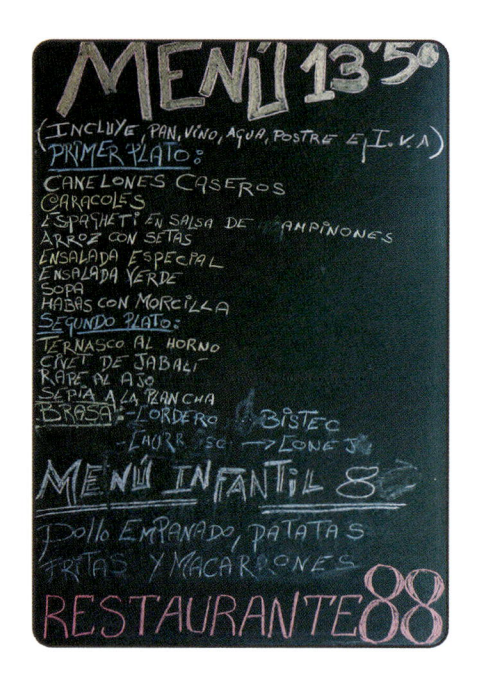

High on my list of all-time favourite eating places is Restaurante 88 in Aragón: to be precise, in Ainsa. From time to time when eating there, I may, vary my choice for the second course, but never the first: it's always caracoles done in 88's, oh so tasty, style. Of all the ways of preparing snails, this is my absolute favourite.

I'm so grateful to the owners, Josep and Alex, for giving me the recipe - especially now that I live on the otherside of the Pyrenees and cannot visit 88 as often as I would like. Now, I can at least conjure up this dish, and with it, memories of the bustle, music and warmth of this happy little restaurant.

This is the method Josep and Alex were taught by Josep's mother; Señora Rosario - from the village of Salás near Tremp. It is a recipe handed down through generations of her family and completely captures the honest flavours of simple dishes, so valued in their traditional food.

Ingredients for 1.:

40 to 50	Snails - helix aspersa - confined as per page 11.
350ml	Beef stock made using one 28g carton of 'Knorr Beef Stock Pot'. *
4 tablespoons	Extra virgin olive oil.
40 - 50ml	Coñac.
2	Dried chillis.
1½ teaspoons	Freshly ground black pepper.
1 teaspoon	Sea salt - if using fine table salt, use less.

* Use this type in preference to 'Knorr Rich Beef Stock Pot' - by the way, I'm not sponsored by Knorr or any other supplier. Use of this brand will give the recipe a close, almost identical result, as you would get in 'Restaurant 88'.

Preparation:

Note: To achieve the correct result, it is important that for the preparation you do no more (or less) than listed below.

1. In fresh cold water, give the snails a thorough washing. Then, rinse and drain them.
2. Sprinkle them with a tablespoon of fine salt and a tablespoon of white wine vinegar.
3. Leave them for 5 minutes and then gently rub them together - this encourages them to give up some of their mucus.
4. Wash them well. Give them a good rinsing two or three times. Drain them once more and they are ready for cooking.

The Snail Cookbook - Walter Gunn

Garden snails a la restaurant 88 Ainsa - serves 1 to 2 as a starter

Cooking:
1. Over a very low heat, put the washed snails into a sauté, or frying, pan and add the olive oil – making sure each snail is well coated.
2. When the heads of the snails have emerged from their shells, raise the heat to medium/high and sprinkle them with the salt – this is the most important moment in the whole process. This is when the snails give up their meaty juices and give the dish its characteristic flavour.
3. Cook at a high heat for 5 minutes while the sauce acquires a khaki like colour.
4. Add the dried chillis, and sprinkle the black pepper over the snails – this is when it acquires its piquancy.
5. Lower the heat a little and leave to cook for another 5 minutes. When the sauce starts to reduce, add the coñac, and without flaming, leave cooking until the coñac has evaporated.
6. Add the stock, raise the heat to high, and bring back to the boil.
7. Reduce the heat and adjust it to maintain a steady low simmer for 1 hour – adding a little more stock, or water, if the dish begins to dry out.
8. Remove from the heat and leave to rest for at least 5 minutes.
9. Serve with alioli or one of the garlic mayonnaises from pages 52 to 55.

The Spanish side - Caracoles en salsa aragonesa

Ingredients - Final cooking:

40 to 50	Snails - helix aspersa - confined and cleaned as per pages 11. to 13. and pre-cooked using Method 2. as described on page 16.
50 to 60g	Onion - finely chopped.
100g	Tomatoes - roughly chopped.
2	Cloves of garlic - finely chopped.
100g	Bacon pieces - green, not smoked.
100g	Chorizo - chopped into small chunks. - see 'Which Chorizo': P. 28
1	Bay leaf.
1	Dried chilli - cut into 4 pieces.
½ teaspoon	Paprika.
1 tablespoon	Flour.
6 tablespoons	Reserved stock from the initial cooking.
150ml	Dry white wine.
2 tablespoons	Extra virgin olive oil.
4 tablespoons	Water.
1 tablespoon	Parsley - chopped fine.
1 teaspoon	Sea salt - if using fine table salt, use less.
Option:	4 tablespoons of Sofrito - see pages 64 to 65.

The Snail Cookbook - Walter Gunn

Garden snails in aragonese sauce - Serves 2 as a main course

This is a wonderful combination of caracoles, spicy chorizo and dried chilli. And, if cooked over a sweet wood-smoke scented fire, it seems to capture the very essence of rich Aragonese mountain food.

I once cooked this recipe outside, over an open fire, on a nose-nipping autumn evening. As always; it would be ridiculous to think otherwise, there were enough glasses of rich, local Somontano vino tinto going down. I do not know of a better way of enjoying this warming, richly flavoured dish.

Such is life in Alto Aragón; a life lived with the word *monotone* deleted from its lexicon.

Final Cooking:

1. Put the olive oil into a sauté pan over a medium heat.
2. Add the onion and garlic, and sauté until beginning to colour.
3. Add the chorizo pieces and chopped bacon, and when they begin to brown nicely, add the flour and paprika and cook for 1 minute.
4. Add the white wine and 6 tablespoons of stock reserved from the initial cooking, and fast simmer for 2 minutes.
5. Lower the heat to medium/low, give all a good stir, then add the chopped tomatoes, bay leaf and salt, and cook slowly for 15 minutes. If using the Sofrito option, add it here.
6. Raise the heat to medium high, add the snails, salt, plenty of grindings of black pepper, the dried chilli and parsley. When the sauce begins a lively simmer, cook for 2 minutes at this pace.
7. Reduce the heat to low, cover, and giving all an occasional stir, cook for another 15 minutes.
8. Check seasoning, take off the heat, and leaving it covered, allow to rest for 10 minutes.
9. Serve with alioli or one of the garlic mayonnaises from pages 52 to 55.

The Spanish side - Caracoles con conejo

Rabbit is one of my favourite meats - it's so versatile - and when coupled this way with caracoles, there is a near perfect marriage of flavours.

Life in the Aragonese mountains was never easy; things didn't get better in the Spanish Civil War when the sweet natured General Franco did all he could to bomb and starve the Aragonese into submission. How welcome the odd rabbit and a sackful of caracoles must have been in those years.

I suspect, that the snails found their way into the recipe to make the rabbit go further. Port and coñac were probably added when times were a little more provident.

This dish is beautifully rich, and if you can't face eating caracoles, then do try it without them - either way, you'll love it.

Ingredients - Final cooking:

1	Rabbit - jointed and chopped into small chunks.
40 to 50	Snails - helix aspersa - confined and cleaned as per pages 11. to 13. and pre-cooked using Method 2. as described on page 16.
1	Onion - finely chopped - about 175g.
1	Green pepper - chopped into roughly 1cm chunks.
4	Tomatoes - roughly chopped - approx 250g.
4	Cloves of garlic - finely chopped.
1 teaspoon	Dried thyme.
1 teaspoon	Dried oregano.
1	Bay leaf.
2	Dried chillis.
250ml	Chicken stock.
200ml	Dry white wine.
150ml	Coñac.
50ml	Port.
6 tablespoons	Extra virgin olive oil.
1 teaspoon	Sea salt - if using fine table salt, use less.

The Snail Cookbook - Walter Gunn

Garden snails with rabbit – serves 2 to 3 as a main course

Final Cooking:
1. Season the rabbit with a sprinkling of salt, and in a sauté pan over a med to high heat, sauté the rabbit in all the olive oil.
2. When the rabbit has taken on a good colour, pour in the coñac and flame.
3. Remove the rabbit from the pan, and in the same oil, sauté the bacon, onion, garlic, thyme and dried chilli, until the onion softens and starts to take on a little colour.
4. Add the green pepper, chopped tomatoes, bay leaf, oregano and the teaspoon of salt, then, sauté over a medium heat for 5 mins.
5. Reserve the liver for later, and return the rest of the rabbit to the pan.
6. Add the white wine and fast simmer for 3 minutes.

7. Add the snails and chicken stock, and simmer for 5 more mins.
8. In a mortar, gently pound the liver and port together, and add to the pan.
9. Give everything a good stir, and gently simmer over a low to medium heat for a further 5 mins.
10. Check seasoning, take off the heat, cover and leave to rest for at least 10 mins.
11. Serve with alioli or one of the garlic mayonnaises from pages 52 to 55.

The Spanish side - Caracoles a la plancha

George Orwell writes in 'Homage to Catalunia' - *'Peasant lads went out with buckets hunting for snails, which they roasted alive on sheets of tin'*. Despite the title of the book referring to Cataluña, at the time of the incident George Orwell was fighting in the Spanish Civil War just outside Huesca in Aragón. It was there, that he was shot in the neck and hospitalised for some considerable time in nearby Barbastro. While on the subject of Barbastro, in this little town I once had one of the finest meals I have ever eaten; made somewhat more memorable by being presided over by the restaurante's 104 year old lady owner.

Roasted over an open fire is by far the simplest method of cooking snails, and ignoring the sheet of tin, archeological digs worldwide show they were prepared this way by early man. See these two recipes as an opportunity to get in touch with your prehistoric side.

Ingredients:
- 20 to 25 Snails – helix aspersa.
- Unsalted butter.
- Garlic.
- Olive oil.
- Sea salt – if using fine table salt, use less.
- Black pepper – freshly ground.
- Chilli powder or sauce.
- Broad-leaved parsley – finely chopped.

Optional accompaniments:
1. A dressing of 1 tablespoon of olive oil, 1 finely chopped clove of garlic, a pinch of sea salt and a tablespoon of finely chopped broad-leaved parsley.
2. 25 to 30g of unsalted butter, 1 teaspoon of finely chopped broad-leaved parsley, a pinch of salt, a grinding of pepper, a pinch of finely chopped garlic and a tiny pinch of chilli powder – or sauce, all mixed together thoroughly.
3. A healthy portion of alioli or one of the garlic mayonnaises from pages 52 to 55.

Preparation:
1. Confine the snails as instructed on page 11.
2. Wash them briefly in cold water with a handful of salt added.
3. Wipe them with a clean cloth.

Note:
1. With this recipe, the snails do not need pre-cooking and require only a brief washing.

The Snail Cookbook - Walter Gunn

Roasted garden snails serves 2 as a light tapa

Cooking method 1.
1. Put the snails, opening uppermost, on a parilla, plancha — which is just a piece of tin with the sides bent up, a grill or piece of corrugated steel — you get the picture; use what you can get your hands on.
2. Place the snails, and whatever you are going to cook them on, over a fired-up barbecue or open fire.
3. When their foaming is at a maximum, into the opening of each snail put a good pinch of sea salt, a dribble of olive oil and a grinding of black pepper.
4. Roast them for around 20 to 25 minutes and when the foaming ceases and the meat has separated from the shell, they are done.
5. Serve as they come or with any of the suggested accompaniments.

Cooking method 2.
1. Cover a flat piece of tin or the grooves in a piece of corrugated steel, with a thick layer of coarse sea salt — around 3mm.
2. Place the snails face-down onto the salt and roast them for around 20 to 25 minutes.
3. Wipe each of the snails and turn them face-up and into the opening put a little salt, pepper, crushed garlic and a drop of olive oil. Roast them for a further 2 to 3 minutes.

The Spanish side - Caracoles con chorizo, manzana y sidra

Though this dish has a distinct Basque feel to it, it is nevertheless, in part, a concoction of my own. The roots of this dish are indeed deeply embedded in the Basque country - the cider there is as good as anything you'll find in England and their sausages are legend. Traditionally, the recipe uses only chorizo, cider and a small splodge of olive oil. This more elaborate version of my own includes apples - cox's are perfect - demerara sugar, and of course snails. It is ready to serve when the cider has almost totally evaporated and the juices from the apples, chorizo, olive oil and sugar have combined into a delicious syrup.

Which Chorizo? A point worth mentioning when buying chorizos is that they come in two forms; one is dried and used thinly sliced as a tapa - this is the firmer of the two and to preserve them, they contain a lot of salt; far too much for cooking. The other, much softer, is the type you need with recipes in this book - much less salt is used in their making, so they are usually stored in the fridge. Unless you want to ruin whatever you are cooking, it is advisable, never to substitute one for the other.

Ingredients:

30	Garden snails - helix aspersa - confined and cleaned as per pages 11. to 13. and pre-cooked using Method 2. as described on page 16.
150 - 175g	Chorizo sausages cut into approx 1 cm pieces.
1 large	Apple - Cox's will do fine - peeled, cored and cut into segments.
250ml	Dry cider - that is, really dry.
1 tablespoon	Extra virgin olive oil.
1 teaspoon	Demerara sugar.

The Snail Cookbook - Walter Gunn

Garden snails with chorizo, apple and cider
serves 1 as a main course or 2 as a starter

Cooking:
1. Put the olive oil into frying pan over a medium heat.
2. Add the chopped chorizo pieces and sauté them for around 5 minutes until they are turning colour nicely.
3. Add to the chorizo the pre-cooked snails in their shells and continue to cook for a further 4-5 minutes, turning them over carefully from time to time.
4. Add the apple segemnts and sprinkle the sugar over all.
5. Add the cider and cook until the liquid has reduced to at least a quarter of its original volume, and a delicious and thick sauce results.
6. Check for salt, give a few good grindings of black pepper, and serve with crusty fresh bread.

The Spanish side - Caracoles con tomillo y perejil

Always, I associate this recipe with springtime in the Aragonese village of Coscojuela de Sobrarbe. It was there, at that beautiful old house, Casa Sarrato, with its warren of arched bodegas and passages leading off in every direction, that I first cooked 'Snails and Thyme'. It is springtime when the light is crystal clear. It has that lucid, contrasty quality artists are forever seeking, when colours are brightened, not dampened by the sun, and everything looks freshly opened. The days are warm and wild herbs are growing everywhere. This is the time of year that snails, having stuffed themselves on all those herbs, are plumping up - in my opinion, it is also the time that their flavour is at its best. Whether it's a coincidence or not, their shells also seem to be in their best condition; shiny, with toffee-like contrasting blacks and browns.

Ingredients - Final cooking:

40 to 50	Snails - helix aspersa - confined and cleaned as per pages 11. to 13. and pre-cooked using Method 2. as described on page 16.
50 to 60g	Onion - finely chopped.
2	Cloves of garlic - finely chopped.
1 teaspoon	Dried thyme.
1	Bay leaf.
1 tablespoon	Chopped fresh parsley.
1	Dried chilli.
4 tablespoons	Extra virgin olive oil.
150ml	Dry white wine.
4 tablespoons	Reserved liquid from initial cooking.
1 teaspoon	Sea salt - if using fine table salt, use less.

The Snail Cookbook - Walter Gunn

Garden snails with thyme and parsley – serves 1 as a starter or main course

Final Cooking:
1. Put the olive oil in a sauté pan over a medium heat, and sauté the onion, garlic, thyme, bay leaf and dried chilli, until the onion starts to take on a golden colour.
2. Raise the heat to medium high and add the snails. Sauté them in the onion and herb mixture for 5 mins.
3. Add the white wine and fast simmer for 2 minutes.
4. Add the remaining ingredients, lower the heat, and with the occasional stir, simmer for 5 minutes more.
5. Remove from the heat and allow to rest for at least 5 minutes.
6. Serve with alioli or one of the garlic mayonnaises from pages 52 to 55.

The Spanish side - Caracoles con chocolata

It's an odd point of history that the part of Flanders that was to become Belgium - euro destination for all discerning chocolate eaters - should have been notionless that the raw material of their future reputation was in the early 1500s, being melded into delicious savoury dishes just a few hundred miles away in Spain.

Initially introduced as a drink, Spanish passion for this Aztec export, soon saw its use extended into the wider kitchen. Toothsome recipes for partidges, chicken, beef, hare and rabbit, all with chocolate thickened sauces, hit the tables. It is no surprise then, that this passion for things chocolate should have also found its way into snail recipes.

I give the above, to point out that this recipe, and its many variations still cooked today, are not the result of some trendy chef's need for publicity. They have the taste-test of time behind them; and this one is paticularly delicious.

Ingredients:

30 to 40	Snails - helix aspersa - confined and cleaned as per pages 11. to 13. and pre-cooked using Method 3. as described on page 17.
1	Onion - 100g finely chopped weight.
350g	Tomatoes - well ripened and chopped.
1 slice	Bread - good white or wholemeal with crusts - fried - about 30 to 40g.
20 - 25g	Dark chocolate - minimum cocoa butter content 70 or 80% - grated.
20 - 25g	Hazel nuts - raw.
250ml	Chicken stock made using one 28g carton of 'Knorr Chicken Stock Pot'.
50ml	Extra virgin olive oil - for cooking the onion and tomatoes.
1 tablespoon	Extra virgin olive oil - for frying the bread.
1 teaspoon	Sherry vinegar - and maybe a little more when adjusting the balance at the end of cooking.
1 clove	Garlic.
1	Dried chilli.
1	Bay leaf.
2 teaspoons	Flour - plain.
½ teaspoon	Sugar.
½ teaspoon	Sea salt - if using fine table salt, use less.

Preparation:

1. Put the tablespoon of olive oil into a frying pan over a medium heat and fry the slice of bread until it is crisp and golden.
2. Make the Picada by finely chopping together the garlic, nuts, chilli and fried bread, and then, adding the grated chocolate.

The Snail Cookbook - Walter Gunn

Garden snails with chocolate - serves 1 to 2 as a starter

Cooking:

1. In a sauté pan, over a medium/low heat put in the olive oil, the chopped tomatoes, onion, bay leaf, sugar and the salt.
2. Gently simmer the mixture until its volume has reduced by half.
3. Sprinkle in the flour and mix in thoroughly, raise the heat to medium and cook at a good bubble for at least one minute.
4. Add the chicken stock - to avoid lumps, stir it into the sauce a little at a time.
5. Add the snails and one teaspoon of sherry vinegar, coat them generously with the sauce, and with the pan covered, leave them to cook over a low heat for 20 minutes - if the sauce begins to look a little dry, add a couple of tablespoons of water; repeating this as necessary.
6. Add the Picada to the snails, and after stirring it in gently but thoroughly, cook for another 20 minutes with the pan covered.
7. Check for salt and sherry vinegar - a nice option at this point, is to add a teaspoon of finely chopped fresh mint before serving.

The Snail Cookbook

The Snail Cookbook - Walter Gunn

Recipes from the French side of the Pyrenees:

Garden snails with:

    Bacon - smoked, white wine and parsley butter   34 - 35

    Blue cheese, white wine and garlic, on a bed of mashed potatoes   36 - 37

Roman snails with:

    Butter, almonds and lemon stuffing   38 - 39

    Egg, chillis and breadcrumbs - deep fried   40 - 41

    Lemon and eggs - (Sauce Poulette)   42 - 43

    Lemon and oregano sauce, and crème fraîche   44 - 45

    Parsley and garlic butter stuffing   46 - 47

The French side - Les petit-gris aux lardons

Les petit-gris aux lardons lie well to the plus side of my richness datum, and it is for that reason I recommend the quantities given here, as being plenty for 2 to 3 people as a starter. This should not be inferred as a deterrent to cooking them. If your tastes are for the rich, and you've yet to succumb to gout, dive right in and eat the lot yourself - it makes, take my word for it, a very delicious plateful.

If you do elect to go solo on this one, try serving it with mashed potatoes, or plain boiled rice - you'll find they make for an improved balance. If you haven't the time for potato or rice, then serve with hunks of crusty bread the result is equally acceptable.

Ingredients:

30	Garden snails - helix aspersa - confined and cleaned as per pages 11. to 13. and pre-cooked using Method 1, as described on page 14 to 15.
100g	Bacon pieces - smoked.
75-100g	Onion - finely chopped.
250ml	Dry white wine.
50g	Parsley and garlic butter see pages 56 to 57.
1 tablespoon	Parsley - broad leaved, or chervil - finely chopped.
1 tablespoon	Extra virgin olive oil.
	Freshly ground black pepper.
	Sea salt.

Preparation:

1. Make the parsley and garlic butter, and then form into walnut sized knobs. Leave them to cool in the refrigerator - do not do this too far in advance as the garlic will lend a rancid tone to the butter.
2. With a tooth-pick, or cocktail stick, remove the pre-cooked snails from their shells or if they were frozen after pre-cooking, de-frost them. Should you have managed to find them in tins; rinse them.

Garden snails with bacon - serves 2 to 3 as a starter

Cooking:
1. On a low/med heat, simmer the shelled snails in 125g of the dry white wine for 6 to 7 minutes, or until the wine has evaporated.
2. Remove the snails and set aside.
3. In the same pan, dry fry the bacon pieces in their own fat until they are lightly browned, and then set them aside.
4. Add the olive oil. Over a low/medium heat, gently sweat the chopped onions and garlic until soft; without allowing them to colour.
5. Add the snails and bacon to the onion and garlic mix.
6. Pour in the remaining 125g of dry white wine, and simmer for 8 to 10 minutes over a low heat.
7. One by one, add the walnut sized knobs of parsley butter, and mix in to form the sauce.
8. Add a few grindings of freshly milled black pepper, and check the sauce for salt.
9. Sprinkle over the tablespoon of finely chopped chervil or parsley and serve still sizzling hot, accompanied by fresh chunks of French bread and a good red wine.

The French side - Les petis gris au roquefort

This is a nice twist on a recipe one comes across fairly regularly in France. Normally, the pre-cooked snails, served in individual earthenware dishes with their cooking sauce, are covered with slices of Roquefort blue cheese and placed in a very hot oven for a few minutes.

Traditional as the above may be, I much prefer the way I suggest here: the pre-cooked snails, once removed from their shells, are sautéed in a sauce of butter, shallots, garlic, parsley and black pepper. The pan is finally, and deliciously, deglazed with dry white wine.

The empty shells have a little blue cheese and butter mixture pushed into them, the sautéed snails are replaced on top of this, and then more of the mixture is pushed into the mouth of the shell. The snails are then grilled, mouth uppermost, on a bed of mashed potatoes until the butter and blue cheese melts. And, while this is being done, the remainder of the cheese and butter is melted into the sauce, which is then reduced until it is of a nice dipping consistency.

When the grilling is done, the sauce is poured over the snails and mashed potatoes; and very tasty it is too.

Ingredients:

25 to 30	Garden snails - helix aspersa - confined and cleaned as per pages 11. to 13. and pre-cooked using Method 1, as described on page 14 to 15.
1	Shallot - finely chopped.
1 clove	Garlic - finely chopped.
100ml	Dry white wine.
50g	Butter - unsalted.
50g	Blue cheese - Roquefort is more authentic.
	Mashed potato - enough to cover the base of the dish by 1 to 2 cm.
2 teaspoons	Parsley - broad leaved - finely chopped.
	Freshly ground black pepper - a few twists of the pepper mill.
	Sea salt - a good pinch.

Preparation:

1. Pre-cook the snails as given on page... and with a toothpick remove them from their shells - you can, should you wish to, remove the dark lower intestine. This is often done in France but not in Spain.
2. Warm the butter until it is workable without being too soft. Blend together the butter and cheese, form into hazel nut sized knobs, and leave them to cool in the refrigerator - it handles better this way when filling the shells.
3. While the snails are being sautéed - see opposite page - put a little of the butter/cheese mix into each of the empty shells.
4. Steam and mash the potatoes, and with them, cover the bottom of an oven-proof dish and keep warm.

The Snail Cookbook - Walter Gunn

Garden snails with blue cheese - serves 2

Cooking:

1. In a pan on a medium/low heat, melt the butter, add the pinch of salt and sauté the pre-cooked snails for 5 minutes.
2. Add the shallots and sauté for a further 5 minutes.
3. Add the garlic and parsley to the pan and sauté for another 2 minutes.
4. Add a few grindings of freshly ground black pepper, and with the wine, deglaze the pan for 2 minutes more.

5. Remove the snails from their sauce and place on top of the cheese/butter in their shells – see note Roman snails, parsley & garlic butter, cooking, point 5.
6. Fill the remaining space in the shells with butter and cheese until it is level with their mouths.
7. Push the filled shells, mouths uppermost into the mashed potatoes – this will hold the snails upright and prevent their contents spilling out.
8. Place them into a pre-heated oven – 235°C Gas mark 7. – until the butter and cheese have melted and is browning nicely.
9. While the snails are in the oven, add the remaining butter/cheese mix and any bits of snail left over to the sauce and over a medium heat reduce until it reaches a nice dipping consistency.
10. When the snails are done, pour the sauce over the snails and potato, and serve piping hot.

The French side - Escargots aux amandes et citron

Almonds in the stuffing, and toasted almonds scattered over the finished dish. It is only the butter that marks it a French recipe. Otherwise, this could easily be thought to come from the Spanish side of the border. It is actually from Provence, where I once spent an afternoon next to blooming lavender fields bordered by almond trees.   Using stones as anvils, and stones as hammers, we sat on the ground and cracked open the green nuts. Their flavour exquisite; the experience; ancient.

The stuffing is original; the rice a personal whim.

The Snail Cookbook - Walter Gunn

Roman snails stuffed with butter, almonds and lemon - serves 1

Ingredients:

12	Roman snails - helix pomatia - tinned or frozen.
	or
25	Common garden snails - helix aspersa - confined and cleaned as per pages 11. to 13. and pre-cooked using Method 1, as described on page 14 to 15.
1	Shallot - 30g finely chopped and peeled weight.
30g	Almonds - peeled.
20g	Almonds - peeled, finely chopped and toasted.
2 cloves	Garlic - crushed.
1 tablespoon	Parsley - broad leaved.
60g	Butter.
1 tablespoon	Lemon juice - fresh.
	Freshly ground black pepper.
	Sea salt.
	Boiled long grain rice cooked as described on pages 62 to 63.

Preparation:

1. If using cleaned and confined common garden snails see pages: 11, 12 and 13. Pre-cook them as instructed by Method 1. (courte bouillon) pages: 14 and 15. With a toothpick, remove the snails from their shells - you can, should you wish to, remove the dark lower intestine. This is often done in France but not in Spain.
2. Cook the rice as instructed on pages 62 to 63.
3. Over a good flame, toast the almond pieces in a small non-stick pan until they have taken on a nice dark colour.
4. Warm the butter until it is soft and workable; workable is the word, not too soft.
5. Blend together all the ingredients except: the snails, toasted almonds and rice.
6. Stuff a little of the mixture, followed by a snail, into each of the shells and finally cap with a generous layer of the stuffing mix.

Cooking:

1. Put an even layer of the cooked rice into an oven proof dish, and on it place the filled shells, mouths uppermost.
2. Dot pieces of the remaining butter-stuffing on the rice.
3. Place under a hot grill for 5 - 8 minutes or until the stuffing melts and bubbles out of the shells.
4. Sprinkle over all, the toasted chopped almonds, and serve piping hot.

The French side - Friture d'escargots

If you do, hot and spicy, do try this with the fresh chilli option. In France, the near mythical 'Piment d'Esplette' would be used - it would be added to the breadcrumbs. As you are unlikely to easily find it, and I cannot see any point in making life more difficult than it already is, I suggest you use dried chillis instead; frying them in the oil first. If, like myself, you choose to eat the snails with a squeeze of lemon, mayo and fresh chilli, trust me: you'll never tell the difference.

This dish encourages bad habits - as in, eating more of it than is decent - and is best eaten accompanied by a young chilled red wine or a good cold Belgian beer.

Ingredients:

12	Roman snails - helix pomatia - tinned or frozen - shells are not used.
	or
25	Common garden snails - helix aspersa - confined and cleaned as per pages 11. to 13. and pre-cooked using Method 1, as described on page 14 to 15.
1	Egg yolk.
3 tablespoons	Breadcrumbs - use good white bread a day or so old and don't make them too fine. This way the coating will be much crunchier.
2	Dried chillis - guindillas.
	Olive oil - enough to cover the base of the cooking pan by 1cm.
½ teaspoon	Sea salt.
	A couple of wedges of fresh lemon.

Options:

1	Fresh chilli - red or green sliced into thin rings.
	A dollop of garlic mayo or all-i-oli described on pages 52 to 55.

Preparation:

1. Defrost, or de-can, and rinse the snails or, if using the common garden snail, prepare and use pre-cooking Method 1, the classic courte-bouillon - see pages 14 to 15.
2. Drain and dab the snails dry.
3. In a shallow dish beat the egg yolk and add the snails coating them well.
4. Spread the breadcrumbs on a large plate and mix in the salt.
5. Ready the lemon wedges.

Roman snails deep fried in egg and breadcrumbs - serves 1

Cooking:
1. Put the oil into a small saucepan over a medium/high heat and allow it to get very hot — test the temperature by putting in a small pinch of the breadcrumbs. They should take on colour in a few seconds.
2. Add the dried chillis and allow them to fry for a couple of minutes — so that their potency is donated to the oil.
3. Roll the egg-covered snails in the breadcrumbs and put, a few at a time, into the hot oil — too many at one time, will reduce the heat of the oil and the resulting crust will be soggy.
4. Fry until the coating is nicely golden.
5. Serve hot with a squeeze of lemon, mayo and a few fresh chilli rings — blisteringly good.

The French side - Escargots sauce poulette

Ingredients - Cooking the snails:

24	Roman snails - helix pomatia - tinned or frozen - their shells are not used.
	or...
	45 to 50 Garden snails - confined and cleaned as per pages 11. to 13. and pre-cooked using Method 1, as described on page 14 to 15.
1	Shallot - finely chopped - about 40g peeled and chopped weight.
1 clove	Garlic - crushed.
1 small sprig	Thyme - a pinch will do if using dried thyme.
25g	Butter - unsalted.
150ml	Dry white wine.
	Freshly ground black pepper - a few good grindings to taste.
	Sea salt - to taste.

Ingredients - The sauce:

2	Fresh egg yolks.
2 tablespoons	Chicken stock - use a small pinch of a stock cube and boiling water.
2 tablespoons	Lemon juice - fresh.
2 tablespoons	Crème fraîche or double cream.
1 tablespoon	Broad leaved parsley - finely chopped.
1 teaspoon	Cornflour.

The Snail Cookbook - Walter Gunn

Roman snails with lemon and egg sauce - serves 2

This marriage of *'Sauce Poulette'* and escargots, is right up to the mark. In the manner I usually cook it; with crème fraîche, it lends a tartness that nicely balances the sweetness of the shallots. If however, you elect to use the cream option, it is best to lower the intensity of the garlic by removing its centre 'germ' if it is present - it is this, from which the garlic will throw out a fresh shoot later in the season. The germ has greater potency than the rest of the clove, and French chefs remove it when the sauce is of a delicate nature. As point of interest, this advice was also given to me by a Spanish acquaintance, when he was making all-i-oli. If you have ever tried pukka all-i-oli, you will realise that this bit of reasoning is redundant. All-i-oli being so fearsome, I fail to understand how one could tell the difference.

Preparation:

1. Defrost, or de-can, and rinse the snails or, if using the common garden snail, confine and clean them as per pages 11, 12 and 13. Then pre-cook using Method 1, the classic court-bouillon – see pages 14-15.
2. Prepare the shallot and garlic – remove the centre shoot of the garlic before crushing.
3. Make up the chicken stock, and when cool, add the cornflour and mix until it is without lumps.
4. Mix together well the egg yolks and lemon juice.

Cooking the snails:

1. In a small pan over a low heat, melt the butter. To it, add the chopped shallot and gently sauté until soft and taking on light colour.
2. Add the thyme and the crushed garlic and continue sautéing gently for 2 to 3 minutes.
3. Raise the heat to medium/low, add the snails and stir in well with the mixture.
4. Add a good pinch of salt and several grindings of freshly milled black pepper – leave to simmer for 5mins, then sprinkle over the white wine and allow this to reduce by half.
5. Put the snails and shallot mixture onto a pre-warmed serving dish and keep warm.

Making the sauce:

6. In another pan over a low/medium heat, pour in the stock and cornflour mixture and cook at a gentle simmer until thick and smooth – this takes about a minute.
7. Mix in the crème fraîche, bring to a good simmer and remove from the heat.
8. Off the heat, add the yolk and lemon juice mixture and whisk in well.
9. Check for seasoning, and pour the sauce over the snails in their serving dish.
10. Sprinkle over the finely chopped parsley and serve with plenty of crusty bread.

The French side - Escargots au citron et origan

It was a warm September day and August's harsh heat had slid back over the border into Spain, We had just plaited our garlic crop, and the Greek oregano had that quality that can only be captured by hot summer months. It was the perfect moment to cook this oh so acceptable recipe - I cannot unlink the memory of the day and the dish.

Escargots au citron et origan, has a distinct Mediterranean edge to it. Only the addition of crème fraîche renders it French and not Greek. In Greece, the ubiquitous marriage of olive oil, lemon and oregeno is referred to as the second Holy Trinity. Try this and you'll understand why.

Ingredients:

24	Roman snails - helix pomatia tinned or frozen - shells are not used.
	or
40 to 50	Garden snails - helix aspersa - confined and cleaned as per pages 11. to 13. and pre-cooked using Method 1, as described on page 14 to 15.
2 slices	Smoked bacon - generously thick - around 150-170g for the two.
2 cloves	Garlic - crushed.
1 teaspoon	Greek Oregano - fresh and finely chopped.
1 tablespoon	Olive oil - extra virgin.
2 wedges	Lemon - fresh.
2 tablespoons	Crème Fraîche.
	Freshly ground black pepper - a few good grindings to taste.
	Sea salt - to taste, though with this dish usually not necessary.

Preparation:

1. This is a quick dish to cook, so get everything ready before the kick-off.
2. Defrost, or de-can, and rinse the snails.
3. Crush the garlic.
4. Chop the oregano.
5. Cut the lemon wedges.
6. Crème Fraîche at the ready.

The Snail Cookbook - Walter Gunn

Roman snails with lemon and oregano – serves 2

Cooking:
1. In a frying pan over a medium heat, fry the bacon in the olive oil until it starts to colour, then remove it and set aside, keeping it warm.
2. Add the snails to the fat and oil the bacon has been cooked in and sauté them for 5 minutes – avoid letting them stick to the bottom of the pan.
3. Add the crushed garlic and chopped oregano, and sauté for a further 3 minutes.
4. Lower the heat. Add 1 of the tablespoons of crème fraîche and gently simmer for 2 minutes.
5. Place the snails and their sauce with the bacon, and season with a few grindings of freshly milled black pepper – cooked this way, this recipe rarely needs additional salt.
6. Add the remaining tablespoon of crème fraîche. Squeeze the juice from one of the lemon wedges over the snails – the remaining wedge of lemon is there in case you fancy some more.
7. Serve with chunks of fresh bread.

The French side - Escargots au beurre vert

To deliver a book aimed at the newcomer to French snail cuisine and fail to include this classic recipe, would be missing out a vital element of the country's cuisine. As the snail of choice for this dish, restaurants will serve the Roman Snail - *Helix Pomatia*. This version of the classic recipe, was given to me by a near neighbour in the Hautes Pyrenees. Although a touch more fiddly, my neighbour, like most other Pyrenean folk, uses 'les petits-gris' - *Helix Aspersa*. This makes sense; they are free, have a better flavour and will ruin your garden if they are not eaten - often.

There are many variations of parsley and garlic butter, these use a variety of herbs, nuts, anchovies and sometimes a few scrapings of nutmeg. All the same, this is the classic version and we'll stick with it - we'll even use the larger Roman snail.

To prevent the snails from toppling over and spilling out their contents whilst cooking, special plates with half a dozen dimples in them are sold. Another option is to wedge them tightly into an earthenware dish. A much better way than both the previous, and the one I like best, is to push them into slices of bread. Then, the toasty, herby, buttery bread is eaten as a scrunchy, delicious accompaniment.

Ingredients for 1:

12   Large snails - helix pomatia - tinned or frozen - their shells are usually packaged seperately.

Preparation:

1. Defrost, or de-can, and rinse both the snails and their shells.
2. Prepare the beurre vert - see pages 56 - 57.
3. Into each of the shells place a little of the butter, then a snail followed by a generous capping of more butter - using force to push the snails into their shells is not the way to do it; it will simply crush them. They need to be almost screwed back into the shell following the shell's natural spiral - for the mechanically minded, they have, in the main, a right-hand thread. Just occasionally, you will come across those with left-hand threads. Butter left over from filling should be spread over the bread.

The Snail Cookbook - Walter Gunn

Roman snails with parsley and garlic butter - serves 1

Cooking:
1. Cover the base of an ovenproof dish with one or two slices of good white bread - crusts included.
2. Make thumb sized dimples in the bread, then place the snails in them with their open end facing upwards and cook under a hot grill for 5 - 7 minutes until the butter is bubbling and browning.
3. Serve, still sizzling hot, accompanied with fresh chunks of French bread and a glass, or two, of good young red wine.

The Snail Cookbook

The Snail Cookbook - Walter Gunn

Sauces and accompaniments from both sides of the Pyrenees:

All-i-oli	50 - 51
A few mayonnaises	52 - 53
Garlic and parsley butter	54 - 55
Lemon and egg sauce - sauce poulette	56 - 57
Potato mayonnaise	58 - 59
Rice - boiled long grain	60 - 61
Sofrito	62 - 63

Sauces and accompaniments

All-i-oli is not garlic mayonnaise. Oh, I'll grant you may hear, or read, of mayonnaise with garlic in it being referred to as 'All-i-oli', but they are not the same thing. That is why, I have given them separate territories. All-i-oli is to mayonnaise, as a wolverine is to a gerbil. True all-i-oli consists of only garlic, olive oil, salt, and occasionally, but not always, a few drops of lemon juice. It never contains egg yolks, mustard - dijon or otherwise, sugar or vinegar. To help the initial stages of emulsification, you may see added a small piece of bread about the size of a walnut, or even a piece of quince - if you want to retain any street-cred at all, don't do this.

It is fearsome stuff. Eat this and your breath can melt plastic for two days afterwards. It is made in a mortar and never a blender; its creation will not allow haste. A traditional porrón is used to deliver the oil. They are designed to do so drop by drop, or to give a thin, steady drizzle from its spout. These are almost indispensable when making all-i-oli – you can use a jug with a thin spout, but they're much less precise, and you'll have to be very careful not to over-pour. It is said by the cognoscenti, that all-i-oli is done, dusted, and ready to serve, only when the pestle can remain standing upright in the mixture without visible support.

There happens to be a curious piece of folk-lore concerning the use of the pestle, it's this; they say, that if while making all-i-oli you start using the pestle in a clockwise, or anti-clockwise, direction, you must continue throughout the entire operation in that same direction. Failure to do so will render disaster. It taking so long to make, I haven't dared; ever, to test my scepticism and buck this piece of wisdom.

What is true for most vegetables is true for garlic; *fresh is best*. In the early part of the year, before the new crop has arrived, garlic often sprouts a small green shoot from its centre. Opinions vary as to whether this be removed. It can taste bitter, and it certainly increases the pungency. With garlic mayonnaises I can see the point: they have a much softer character. With All-i-oli, to leave it out is a bit odd. This is such a *ferocious* beast, and I would have thought subtleties such as this, irrelevant - a bit like the SAS following 'Health and Safety' guidelines.

I have to tell you, this is the hardest thing in the book to get right. The result though, when eaten with snails; of course, cold meats, new potatoes with their skins on, with lamb chops, or those delicious Catalan sausages; *Butifaras*, is outstanding – persevere in making it, and you'll love yourself for doing so.

The Snail Cookbook - Walter Gunn

All-i-oli - as a part of, or accompaniment to, many dishes

Ingredients:
3   Cloves of garlic.
100ml   Extra virgin olive oil.
           A good pinch of sea salt - but less than ¼ of a teaspoon.

Preparation:
1. Raise the oil to room temperature.
2. Raise the mortar and pestle to room temperature.

Making:
1. In a mortar, grind the garlic and salt together to form a smooth paste.
2. Using the pestle in one direction only, and without stopping grinding and turning, pour, drop by drop, the oil onto the edge of the mortar so that it gently runs down the side and into the garlic/salt mixture. When it starts to thicken, then, and only then, can you increase the flow of oil. Keep going until all the oil is used and the pestle, unassisted, is able to stand up in the resulting all-i-oli.

If it all goes wrong:
Recovery is possible and what you end up with will be first class, but, it won't be all-i-oli. Here's what you do...
1. Put the failed all-i-oli into a measuring jug and using sunflower oil, bring the total liquid up to 200ml.
2. Follow the instructions for Mayo 3. in this section, omitting the oil, garlic, and only adding a further ¼ teaspoon of sea salt.

Sauces and accompaniments

I'll leave the origin of mayonnaise to food historians; they still argue about it. The Minorcans, say it was used in Mahon centuries before the French had emerged from the caves at Lasceaux. The French, can't make theirs minds up whether it's name stems from *manier* or *moyeu*. You see what I mean, it's best to leave them to it.

So much has been written on how to recover a curdled mayo. The best way by far, is to not let it happen in the first place. This is as easy to do, as it is to write.

Follow this and you'll never have a mayo crisis; make sure the eggs and oil are at a comfortable room temperature. If you try making any of these mayos with eggs straight from the fridge, you stand a good chance of the mixture curdling; if it doesn't, then there's an equally good chance that your fridge is up-the-shoot.

If your eggs are cold, place them in luke-warm water and leave it to warm up for 10 mins; OK, let's say luke-warm water is just nice and warm to the touch. If you intend using a stone mortar and pestle, make sure these are also warmed.

Where mustard is used, my preference is for the French; Maille's Dijon Fine Mustard. Both Coleman's and Maille's both work well; try them both and decide yourself.

Mayo 1: Softer in nature than the other two mayos due to the use of egg white, as well as yolk, and the absence of garlic.

Ingredients:

1	Whole egg – at room temperature.
1 level teaspoon	Coleman's English Mustard or Maille Dijon Mustard.
200ml	Sunflower oil.
¼ teaspoon	Sea salt – if using fine table salt, use less or to taste.
2 teaspoons	White wine vinegar.

Mayo 2: Heavier duty than Mayo 1. Less so than Mayo 3, but still attention grabbing. Ideal with any amount of dishes: Snails, meat, fish and hot or cold sausages.

Ingredients:

2	Egg yolks – at room temperature.
3 teaspoons	Coleman's English Mustard or Maille Dijon Mustard.
275ml	Sunflower oil.
¼ teaspoon	Sea salt – if using fine table salt, use less or to taste.
½ teaspoon	Sugar.
2 tablespoons	White wine vinegar.
6 or 8	Turns of the black peppermill.

The Snail Cookbook - Walter Gunn

A few mayonnaises – for many dishes; salads, meats and snails

Mayo 3. This is without any doubt my favourite mayo of all time. It goes so perfectly with so many dishes; cole-slaw, grilled lamb chops, fish, but most of all with snails.

Ingredients:

2	Egg yolks – at room temperature.
1 level teaspoon	Coleman's English Mustard powder or ready made.
2	Cloves of garlic.
150ml	Sunflower oil.
50ml	Olive oil – extra virgin.
3 teaspoons	White wine vinegar.
¾ teaspoon	Sea salt – if using fine table salt, use less or to taste.
½ teaspoon	Sugar.

Preparation for mayos 1, 2 and 3:

1. In a bowl of warm water, bring the eggs, still in their shells, to room temperature – about ten minutes.
2. Bring the oil and mixing bowl or whisking goblet to room temp.

Making mayos 1, 2 and 3:

1. If using garlic, grind it together with the salt in a mortar until it forms a creamy, smooth paste.
2. Add all the ingredients except the oil to the whisking goblet.
3. Whisk this mixture together and when it is well combined, continue whisking and slowly pour, in a fine drizzle, the oil.

Sauces and accompaniments

There are many variations of parsley and garlic butter - beurre vert. These use a variety of herbs, nuts, anchovies and sometimes, a few scrapings of nutmeg. This is the classic version though, here we're sticking more-or-less with tradition.

In the list of ingredients, you'll see it is suggested the shallots are finely chopped. This gives a coarser result; the butter stuffing then has a bit more crunch - and this is how I like it. More traditionally, the finished butter is blended to a much finer consistency, and, as with many over-processed foods, tends to lose character.

Ingredients for a single portion of snails:

50g	Butter - unsalted.
1	Shallot - very finely chopped - 20g peeled and chopped weight.
1 clove	Garlic - very finely chopped.
2 tablespoons	Parsley - broad leaved - finely chopped.
2 pinches	Freshly ground black pepper.
2 pinches	Sea salt.

The Snail Cookbook - Walter Gunn

Garlic and parsley butter

Preparation:
1. Mix together the crushed garlic and salt into a fine paste - this is best done in a mortar, though crushed in a small bowl with the back of a wooden spoon will give a good result.
2. Soften the butter over a gentle heat until it is workable but not too soft to handle.
3. Mix the rest of the ingredients together - it is inadvisable to prepare the butter too far in advance; introduced too early, the garlic will turn the butter quite rancid.

Sauces and accompaniments

This marriage of *'Sauce Poulette'* and escargots is right up to the mark. In the manner I usually cook it; with crème fraîche, it lends a tartness that nicely balances the sweetness of the shallots. If however, you elect to use the cream option, it is best to lower the intensity of the garlic by removing its centre 'germ' if it is present - it is from this that the garlic will throw out a fresh shoot later in the season. The germ has greater potency than the rest of the clove. French chefs remove it where the sauce is of a delicate nature. As point of interest, this advice has also been given to me by a Spanish acquaintance when making all-i-oli. If you have ever tried pukka all-i-oli, you will realise that this bit of reasoning is redundant. All-i-oli is so fearsome, I fail to understand how one could tell the difference.

Sauce poulette

Ingredients:

2	Fresh egg yolks.
2 tablespoons	Chicken stock – made with a little of a stock cube.
2 tablespoons	Lemon juice – fresh.
2 tablespoons	Crème fraîche or double cream.
1 teaspoon	Cornflour.

Preparation:

1. Prepare the shallot and garlic – remove the centre shoot of the garlic before crushing.
2. Make up the chicken stock and when cool, add the cornflour and mix until it is without lumps.
3. Mix together well the egg yolks and lemon juice.

Making the sauce:

1. In pan over a low/medium heat, pour in the stock and cornflour mixture and cook at a gentle simmer until thick and smooth – this takes about a minute.
2. Mix in the crème fraîche, bring to a good simmer and remove from the heat.
3. Off the heat, add the yolk and lemon juice mixture, and whisk in well.
4. Check for seasoning and you're there.

Sauces and accompaniments

I would imagine this variation on theme of all-i-oli was originally conceived by some frugal soul desperately trying to make a few meagre ingredients go a long way. However understandable, frugality doesn't always work; but here it does. *Potato and garlic mayonnaise* is perfectly valid; it holds its own very well against traditional all-i-oli and garlic mayonnaises.

It is very Mediterranean. In Spain it is known as Ajoaciete, in Greece it crops up as; Skordalia. It is so good with snails, cold meats and sausage dishes. Try it the next time you have barbecued spare ribs - you may just find you haven't made enough.

The observant amongst you will have noticed that there are two methods given below. The first one is the method used at Ainsa's Snail Fiesta - La Caracolada, and the other has a much more varied texture. I've made Ajoaciete both ways. It's just an opinion you understand, but I have this feeling blenders can be too much of a good thing. They can tend to make things too smooth. So, of the two methods, I prefer the slightly coarser texture of the second. Here, and I accept that it may be my imagination at work, done the second way, I think it also tastes better.

I must be getting soft, I've been quite modest with the amount of garlic suggested - it will take a lot more.

Preparation:

Method 1.

1. Peel, dice and steam potatoes until cooked.
2. Leave the potatoes to cool.
3. Using a blender, mix all the ingredients into a creamy paste.

Method 2.

1. Peel, dice and steam potatoes until cooked.
2. Leave the potatoes to cool.
3. Put the garlic and salt into a mortar and pound it until it forms a smooth paste.
4. Add the potatoes one by one to the garlic and continue to mortar them until they are well mixed though still a little lumpy.
5. Still using the mortar, blend in the egg yolk.
6. Add the olive oil, 25ml at a time, and keep stirring until it is well incorporated into the mixture.

The Snail Cookbook - Walter Gunn

Potato and garlic mayonnaise - enough for a healthy side dish

Ingredients:

400g	Potatoes - peeled weight.
100ml	Extra virgin olive oil.
2	Cloves of garlic.
1	Egg yolk.
1/2 teaspoon	Sea salt - if using fine table salt, use less.

Sauces and accompaniments

The recipe given here will give you long-grain rice cooked to perfection in under half-an-hour. It will have a delightful nutty aspect and its grains will be separate. As a bonus, you will never again need to buy expensive rice to get a first class result.

The method I use is the result of modifying and combining a few ways I've seen used over the years. In one of these, the rice was repeatedly washed and rinsed in cold water until all the external starch had been removed, and the rinsing water ran clear - thus consigning much of its food value down the plug-hole. As far as I could ever make out, this was all undertaken in the effort to stop the grains sticking together. In this, it was successful, though in doing so, it knocked the guts right out of it.

I'd like to lay a ghost; you'll read here and there, that the correct ratio of water to rice is 2:1, or put another way, twice the volume of water to that of rice. This is given as a universal truth. It is though, a generalisation, and one, I can only imagine, engendered by celebrity chefs or people who have not cooked rice very often: and so myths are perpetuated. The amount of water you need to use will very much depend on the type and growing conditions of rice you are cooking; where it is from; whether grown in a good year or bad year, or how old it is. Even taking into consideration these fairly wide variables, I do not know of a single instance where I've followed the so called 2:1 golden rule. As you will see in the instructions for two people, the starting point will be 14ml of boiling water to 9ml of long-grain rice. And, that is that. Try it this way in the first instance, then if you wish, adjust accordingly next time.

The oil used makes a big difference. If you want to tone down the influence imparted by it, you'll find that using sunflower oil might suit the purpose. If however, like myself, you prefer the green nutty flavours given by good extra virgin olive oil, then use that. Whichever oil you decide to use, make sure it is of the highest quality - so little is used per serving, that it's well worth getting the best.

Ingredients:

9ml	Long-grain rice.
14ml	Boiling water.
1 tablespoon	Extra virgin olive oil.
1 teaspoon	Sea salt - if using fine table salt, use less.

Note:

For the quantity given for two people, it is best to use a small saucepan with a well fitting lid. Its base diameter needs to be around 17cm or 7 inches.

The Snail Cookbook - Walter Gunn

Boiled long-grain rice - *easy and delicious - serves 2*

Cooking:
1. Boil more than enough water and have it ready for the next stage.
2. Over a high heat, put the olive oil into a small saucepan and heat it until it's nearly smoking.
3. Add the rice, and stirring, make sure it gets nice and hot and is well coated with the oil.
4. Measure and add the boiling water, being very careful of the quite violent initial reaction. Stir well, making sure that rice grains do not stick to the bottom of the pan.
5. Add the salt, stir in well, and stirring frequently, cook at a fast boil for 3 minutes.
6. Cover the pan, and over the lowest heat, cook for a further 10 minutes – do not stir or remove the lid at this stage.
7. Remove from the heat and briefly take off the lid to let the steam escape – you will notice that the rice's surface will have a slightly pitted look.
8. Replace the lid, and still off the heat, allow to rest for 15 minutes – do not stir or remove the lid at this stage.
9. Just before serving, give the rice a light fluffing-up with a fork.

Sauces and accompaniments

Before sofrito, sauces must have seemed monochromatic; old black and white movies. A good Sofrito implies much more than a sauce of tomatoes, onions, bay leaves and garlic - it points to alchemy. How beautifully the flavours change with time on the stove: the slightly sharp tomatoes blend with the onion, garlic, bay leaves and olive oil, to yield such soft, rich flavours - slow cooking is obviously best with sorcery.

Bay leaves are essential, though often it is difficult to put one's finger on just what their contribution is. Be that as it may, leave them out, and you'll notice their absence immediately. Mildly narcotic, they lend warmth and a flavour softly reminiscent of cloves.

This sofrito freezes really well and will keep in the fridge for several days. When it has cooled after cooking, I put it in freezer bags with 4 heaped tablespoons in each. Although the advice is for slow cooking, try making it in a deep saucepan, and it will take forever. It rids the excess liquid faster, if you use a shallow, wide pan - the larger surface area is important for this. I use a small paella.

Ingredients:

2	400g tins chopped Spanish or Italian tomatoes.
400g	Peeled and finely chopped, sweet Spanish onions.
200ml	Extra virgin olive oil.
1 level teaspoon	Sugar.
1 level teaspoon	Sea salt - if using fine table salt, use less.
1 level teaspoon	Paprika.
2 large	Bay leaves.

Cooking:

1. Put the olive oil, chopped onions, sugar and salt, into a large sauté pan over a medium to low heat.
2. Stirring the mixture frequently, cook the onion until it is tender and slightly golden; almost translucent - this takes from around 15 to 30 minutes depending on the heat setting - the longer you can afford to wait, the better.

The Snail Cookbook - Walter Gunn

Sofrito of onion, tomatoes and bay leaf

Cooking continued...
3. Add the paprika to the onions, mix in well, and fry for another minute.
4. Add the tomatoes and bay leaves.
5. Raise the heat to medium and stirring from time to time, cook for around 20 minutes.
6. The sofrito is ready when the tomato mixture has darkened and has separated from the olive oil, – giving it a slightly curdled look.

Tip: If the onions start to brown, that is, before they are tender and golden, add a dessertspoonful of cold water. This will reduce the heat, provide a drop more liquid, and give them that extra time they obviously need. Repeat this as often as necessary, though it is preferable to cook at a lower heat.

Printed in Great Britain
by Amazon.co.uk, Ltd.,
Marston Gate.